FEMA

Federal Emergency Management Administration

TRISTAN BOYER BINNS

Heinemann Library
Chicago, Illinois

© 2003 Reed Educational & Professional Publishing

Published by Heinemann Library,
an imprint of Reed Educational & Professional Publishing,
Chicago, IL

Customer Service 888-454-2279

Visit our website at www.heinemannlibrary.com

Page Layout by Molly Heron
Photo research by Jessica Clark
Printed and bound in the United States by Lake Book Manufacturing, Inc.

07 06 05 04 03
10 9 8 7 6 5 4 3 2 1

Library of Congress Cataloging-in-Publication Data

Binns, Tristan Boyer, 1968-
 FEMA : Federal Emergency Management Agency / Tristan Boyer Binns.
    p. cm. -- (Government agencies)
Includes index.
 Summary: An introduction to the Federal Emergency Management Agency,
discussing its nature, structure, and responsibilities.
 ISBN 1-58810-502-4 (HC), 1-58810-984-4 (Pbk)
 1. United States. Federal Emergency Management Agency--Juvenile literature. 2. Disaster relief--United States--Management--Juvenile literature. [1. United States. Federal Emergency Management Agency. 2. Disaster relief. 3. Emergency management.] I. Title: Federal Emergency Management Agency. II. Title. III. Series.
 HV555.U6 B55 2002
 363.34'0973--dc21

                              2001006977

Acknowledgments
Cover photograph by Andrea Booher/FEMA News Photo/AP/WideWorld Photos
top corner, even pages, rain cloud illustration by Guy Palm; p. 2 Doug Menuez/PhotoDisc; p. 4 Patricia Brach/FEMA News Photo; p. 5L, 8B, 12R, 13, 14B, 38B, 40, 41 Federal Emergency Management Agency; p. 5R David Teska/FEMA News Photo; p. 6L Lynn Pelham/TimePix; p. 6R Bill Ray/TimePix; p. 7, 18B, 24, 28 Liz Roll/FEMA News Photo; p. 8T Greg E. Mathieson/FEMA News Photo; p. 9, 19, 27B Dave Saville/FEMA News Photo; p. 10 Doug Hill/FEMA News Photo; p. 11 Jason Pack/FEMA News Photo; p. 12T, 15, 16B, 17, 29T, 42 Dave Gatley/FEMA News Photo; p. 14T Frances M. Roberts; p. 16T, 44 Reuters NewMedia, Inc./Corbis; p. 18T Federal Insurance Administration/Federal Emergency Management Agency; p. 20, 21L, 25B, 26, 27T, 29B, 32, 33R, 43B FEMA News Photo; p. 21R Don Jacks/FEMA News Photo; p. 22 Michael Rieger/FEMA News Photo; p. 23, 25TL, 25TR, 33L Andrea Booher/FEMA News Photo; p. 30 Lloyd Cluff/Corbis; p. 31 Dewberry and Davis, LLC; p. 35 National Emergency Training Center; p. 36, 37B, 38T, 38C, 39 Jay Mallin; p. 37T Courtesy of Bold Industries/www.boldindustries.com; p. 43T Roman Bas/FEMA News Photo

Every effort has been made to contact copyright holders of any material reproduced in this book. Any omissions will be rectified in subsequent printings if notice is given to the publisher.

The author and publisher would like to thank the following for their help: Mike Buckley, Holly Harrington, Kirby Kiefer, Bonnie Butler, Dan Summers, Vanessa Villery

Note to the Reader: Some words are shown in bold, **like this.** You can find out what they mean by looking in the glossary.

Contents

Helping with Disasters

Every year, many disasters and emergencies strike the United States. Some are easier to **forecast**, such as hurricanes. But some happen without warning, such as earthquakes. Many are natural disasters, such as floods and tornadoes. Others, like chemical spills and nuclear reactor leaks, are caused by people. No matter how they happen or why, the Federal Emergency Management **Agency,** or FEMA, will be there to help people survive and recover.

The leaders of FEMA report to the president of the United States. When the president decides that an area is a disaster, or when a predictable disaster is about to strike, FEMA moves in to help. During a disaster, FEMA officials help organize the area so people can get the help they need. Normal everyday things we take for granted, such as having food, clean water, and somewhere to sleep, can become hard to come by during a disaster. Taking people who are hurt to a doctor can mean using helicopters or boats. FEMA workers have much experience providing for and helping people in very difficult situations. These workers also make sure that **communications systems** are working so citizens know what has happened and learn what they should do next.

FEMA officials work with communities all over the country, training citizens so they know what to do in an emergency. They also spend a lot of

A FEMA official inspects a home that was **condemned** after severe storms in Oklahoma.

United States Fire Administration training sessions prepare firefighters for community emergencies.

FEMA officials look at property damage after a flood in Davenport, Iowa.

time helping communities prepare for disasters. Sometimes this means making buildings stronger or moving buildings away from dangerous areas. Other times it means teaching people about how to prevent disasters from starting. Fires, for example, are a problem in buildings and in the wild. FEMA runs the United States Fire Administration, which helps train firefighters all over the country.

FEMA also helps people recover from disasters. Often money is needed to rebuild homes. FEMA helps people apply for disaster aid money. It also runs the National Flood Insurance Program, which insures buildings against loss from flooding.

Know It

More than a year and a half before the 2002 Winter Olympics were held in Salt Lake City, Utah, FEMA workers started training programs for Olympic and city workers. More than 1,500 people helped each other learn what to do in case of a train accident, bomb threat, bomb blast, or **hostage crisis.**

FEMA's History

When a large disaster strikes the United States, the **federal** government steps in to help. The first time this happened was in 1803 in New Hampshire after a fire. In the early years of the country, **Congress** had to pass a law to provide help for each disaster. By the 1930s, the government started to plan how to prevent and help during disasters instead of waiting for disasters to strike. Projects to control floods were created. Special groups were set up to help provide money so that roads, bridges, and buildings could be rebuilt after disasters.

In the 1960s and early 1970s, many natural disasters struck the United States. The new Federal Disaster Assistance Administration handled six hurricanes and earthquakes. But many of the necessary jobs and responsibilities were shared by different **agencies.** Some workers worked for the

Hurricane Carla packed winds of 145 miles (233 kilometers) per hour when it slammed into the Texas coast in 1961.

The Alaskan Earthquake of 1964 rocked the state with an 8.4 magnitude on the Richter Scale. In its wake, 131 people were dead and many homes and buildings damaged or destroyed.

federal government, and others worked for states or local communities. When a disaster happened, knowing who was in charge was very confusing.

In 1974, a new law clearly explained what the president must do to declare a disaster. In 1979, President Jimmy Carter created FEMA. FEMA took over most of the other federal disaster programs. FEMA also had responsibility for **civil defense**, or what to do in case of war or an **invasion** of the United States.

Know It

Some disasters cause so much destruction that communities—and sometimes entire states—need federal help. The president of the United States can declare a "presidential disaster." When this is done, the U.S. government provides money and help. FEMA always helps during **presidentially declared disasters**.

Taking care of nuclear and chemical emergencies were a big part of FEMA's first ten years. FEMA helped handle the **toxic** chemicals at Love Canal and the nuclear accident at Three Mile Island, both in New York state. As the agency grew, its responsibilities changed to trying to prevent disasters and making their impact as small as possible. Since 1997, Project Impact has helped communities prepare for disasters before they strike.

Unusual amounts of rainfall during the summer of 1993 in the Mississippi River region resulted in major flooding across the Midwest.

How FEMA Is Organized

The person in charge of FEMA is the director. A deputy director is next in line. A chief of staff reports to the deputy director. The chief of staff is in charge of the seven **directorates** into which FEMA is organized. The **Regional** Operations directorate runs the ten regional offices. The Readiness, Response, and Recovery directorate is responsible for responding to emergencies. This directorate also is in charge of the training center, where FEMA members are taught how to be ready for disasters.

Officials at FEMA headquarters conduct a teleconference with the ten regional offices.

FEMA publishes maps that show where a community's flood hazard areas are and the amount of risk in those areas.

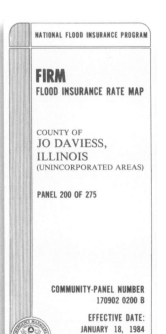

NATIONAL FLOOD INSURANCE PROGRAM

FIRM
FLOOD INSURANCE RATE MAP

COUNTY OF
JO DAVIESS,
ILLINOIS
(UNINCORPORATED AREAS)

PANEL 200 OF 275

COMMUNITY-PANEL NUMBER
170902 0200 B

EFFECTIVE DATE:
JANUARY 18, 1984

Federal Emergency Management Agency

The **Federal** Insurance and **Mitigation** Administration has several responsibilities. One division makes maps that show areas where natural disasters in the United States are likely to happen, such as **floodplains**. These maps help another division plan how to help prevent natural disasters, such as floods, from harming people and places. Both of these divisions are supported by the work of a third division, in which engineers and scientists develop new **technology.** This directorate also runs the National Flood Insurance Program.

The United States Fire Administration runs programs across the country that are designed to help prevent fires and stop people from getting hurt when they do happen. The United States Fire Administration runs the National Fire Academy, which trains and teaches firefighters the best ways to fight fire. It also collects and publishes **statistics** about fires in the United States.

Employees in the External Affairs directorate work with U.S. government officials in the United States and around the world. This directorate is also in charge of the Public Affairs Division. The Public Affairs Division reports news to the media so that citizens know about FEMA's work and **policies.**

Information technology is very important to FEMA, especially when it helps people communicate during an emergency. Workers in the Information Technology directorate keep FEMA computer systems working and develop better ways to communicate.

Workers in the Administration and Resource Planning directorate hire and train new employees. The finance division is in charge of **budgets.**

A search-and-rescue team member saves a stranded dog from flooding that followed Hurricane Floyd in 1999.

Across the United States

FEMA has about 2,600 full-time **employees** working in a number of places. FEMA headquarters is in Washington, D.C. There are offices in each of the ten **regions** across the United States. These offices have between 70 and 115 full-time employees. Smaller area offices fill in between the regional offices. There are two special centers as well.

The National Emergency Training Center in Emmitsburg, Maryland, is where most of the emergency management and fire training courses are held. Workers from outside FEMA go there to learn how to help in an emergency.

FEMA headquarters are located in Washington, D.C.

This map shows FEMA's ten regions, as well as the location of each region's local office.

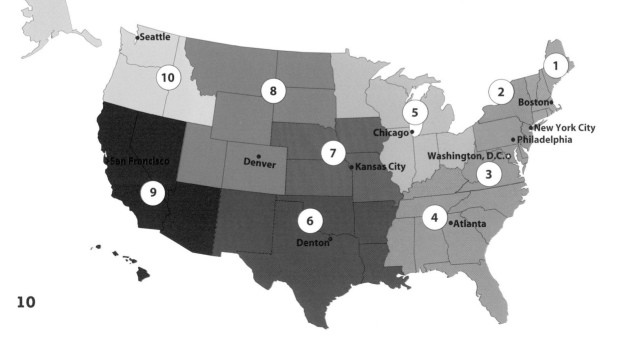

FEMA officials direct emergency response work from the Mount Weather Emergency Assistance Center in Bluemont, Virginia. Different groups of workers help during and after a disaster. One takes phone calls from **victims** asking for help. Another handles the money that is provided after a disaster. Other groups control people and materials that are sent to the scene of a disaster. Computers, other communications equipment, **shelters**, and special clothing all help with the rescue efforts.

During a disaster, specially trained part-time employees join the FEMA team. Up to 4,000 people help on the scene and behind it. Some perform search-and-rescue missions, others answer phones, and some keep communications going. Each regional office can call upon about 200 part-time employees when needed.

More than 80 workers in the FEMA North Carolina Disaster Field Office talk with disaster victims about temporary housing needs. Each FEMA worker contacts about 125 disaster victims every day.

FEMA workers do not handle emergencies and disasters by themselves. They have partnerships with local emergency response teams, such as firefighters, police forces, hospitals, and builders. State **agencies** also work together with local teams and FEMA workers to make sure people are getting the kind of help they need. As many as 28 **federal** agencies may help with disaster efforts. One person is chosen by the president to organize all the federal agencies at the disaster. Together with the state and local teams, they are in charge. FEMA officials also work with the American Red Cross to give good medical help where it is needed.

Reducing the Risk

FEMA officials respond to disasters in carefully planned steps. The first step should be **mitigation**, which means working to make sure disasters have less impact on people and places. Then comes "preparedness," or being prepared when a disaster strikes. After a disaster strikes, the next step is

Houses like this one are built on stilts to protect them from rising waters. The Building Performance Assessment Team (BPAT) helps people build stronger and safer homes.

response. This means getting people and resources to the scene and working quickly to rescue people and make the area safe. The last step is recovery, or helping people rebuild their communities and lives after a disaster. FEMA **employees** help throughout by providing training, money, technical experts, special equipment, and organizing skills. The U.S. government gives FEMA money to help start mitigation work as part of the response and recovery work.

Mitigation means many different things. Because surviving natural disasters often means having a strong

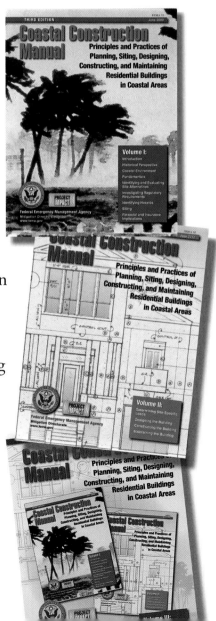

The Coastal Construction Manual helps people who build houses by the coast know what to do to make them stronger in case of floods, hurricanes, earthquakes, or tornadoes.

building to shelter in, mitigation work looks at making stronger buildings. One group of FEMA workers, called the Building Performance Assessment Team, looks at how buildings are destroyed in disasters. Then the team works with builders to build stronger buildings. Another FEMA program teaches people how to make rooms in their houses and offices safer in case of a hurricane or tornado.

FEMA also helps people who live on **floodplains.** The Hazard Mapping Division makes maps of floodplains all across the country. This information is used to help provide flood **insurance.** It also helps the mitigation response by moving buildings that have been built on floodplains.

FEMA to the Rescue!

At the Little Church on the Prairie Learning Center in Lakewood, Washington, FEMA workers helped save and protect the building and children. The center was built in an area that was threatened by earthquakes. FEMA officials worked with the center to make sure that the buildings were strong enough to survive an earthquake. **Volunteers** helped bolt cribs, televisions, computers, and hot water heaters to the walls. Special shields were put over lights so they wouldn't fall and hurt people. When an earthquake did strike, no one was hurt and nothing fell.

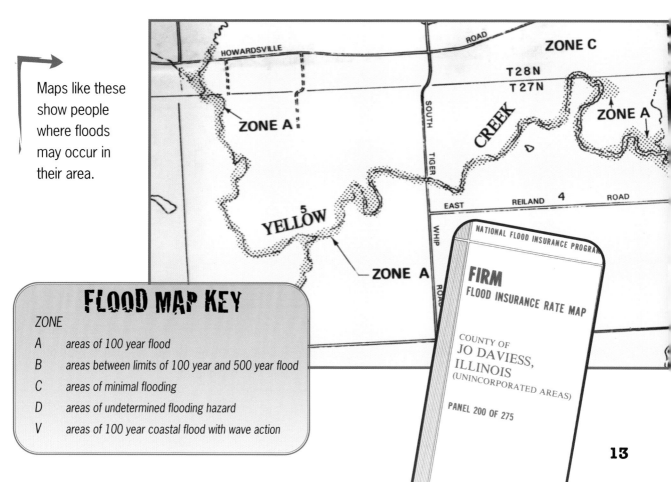

Maps like these show people where floods may occur in their area.

FLOOD MAP KEY

ZONE

A areas of 100 year flood

B areas between limits of 100 year and 500 year flood

C areas of minimal flooding

D areas of undetermined flooding hazard

V areas of 100 year coastal flood with wave action

NATIONAL FLOOD INSURANCE PROGRAM

FIRM
FLOOD INSURANCE RATE MAP

COUNTY OF
JO DAVIESS,
ILLINOIS
(UNINCORPORATED AREAS)

PANEL 200 OF 275

13

Being Prepared

At FEMA, people talk about "preparedness." This means being ready for a disaster. If citizens know what to do if a disaster strikes, they can save lives and **property.** The first step in training people is writing an emergency plan. This plan lists what the community will do in case of different types of disasters. Once the plan is written, citizens are taught special skills to handle many kinds of possible disasters. FEMA workers also teach citizens how to protect themselves at home during a disaster.

Preparedness also means teaching citizens how to rebuild their communities after the danger is past. Citizens even learn how to prevent damage from future problems. FEMA officials organize training classes at its Emergency Management Institute. They also have classes broadcast by **satellite** for people who can't come to the institute.

FEMA works with communities to organize practice exercises, or rehearsals. During these, citizens pretend that a disaster has struck to

Disaster preparedness drills teach emergency workers how to respond to a crisis.

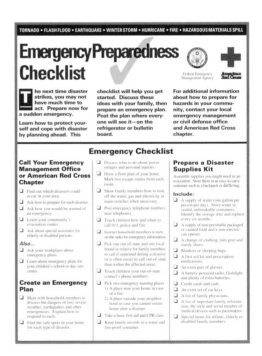

An Emergency Preparedness Checklist can help you and your family plan what to do in case of an emergency.

make sure they know what to do in case of a real emergency. They can then update their plans to make them even better.

FEMA workers also help build emergency operations centers. These are places where efforts are coordinated during a crisis—emergency headquarters! When an disaster hits, FEMA uses special computers and **software** that predict what kind of damage might happen and how many people might be hurt. Workers then use that information to send the right kinds of people and equipment to help. FEMA officials also work with **nuclear power plants** and **hazardous waste** sites to plan how best to react to an emergency.

Project Impact

FEMA officials say that for every dollar spent to prevent disaster damage, two dollars are saved in repairs that aren't needed to rebuild. With this in mind, FEMA officials created Project Impact. Project Impact helps communities prepare for disasters. Local citizens and business owners work together with FEMA to plan and create ways to prevent and minimize the effects of disasters.

A Project Impact worker moves a water heater above ground so it will continue to work during a flood.

A Closer Look: Hurricane Floyd

Two men rescue a cat from a flood caused by Hurricane Floyd in Bound Brook, New Jersey.

In September 1999, Hurricane Floyd began moving up the East Coast of the United States. Before it even touched land, FEMA workers were getting prepared. Workers were ready to help as the disaster happened. Here's what happened:

NEWS BULLETIN
September 13—The Emergency Support Team is called together. Working with different **agencies,** they get ready to handle communications, transportation, fires, medical care, **shelters,** food, and search-and-rescue missions.

NEWS BULLETIN
September 14—FEMA disaster response specialists go to Atlanta, Georgia, to work with the states in the hurricane's path to help prepare. Sites in Georgia, Florida, and South Carolina get ready to help. Doctors, engineers, and clean-up workers are put on alert and move close to where Floyd is expected to strike. **Electric generators,** plastic sheets, tarps, bottled water, food, portable toilets, blankets, cots, sleeping bags, and ice are made available. Almost 15,000 people in Florida were **evacuated** to 64 shelters. The communities in Florida, South Carolina, North Carolina, Virginia, Delaware, and Georgia that are a part of Project Impact are ready for the storm. By the end of the day, 806 **federal** workers are ready.

A few hours before Hurricane Floyd hits Wilmington, North Carolina, most people begin to leave the city.

NEWS BULLETIN

September 15—Hurricane Floyd passes Florida and Georgia without touching land. But it still causes great damage and flooding. President Bill Clinton declares an emergency, and teams prepare to begin their work. Urban Search-and-Rescue Teams and emergency supplies go to Georgia. More than 38,000 people are in 244 shelters in Florida, and more than 6,000 people are in shelters in Georgia and South Carolina. By the end of the day, 2,100 federal workers are involved.

NEWS BULLETIN

September 16—Hurricane Floyd hits land in North Carolina and speeds north through Virginia. It gets weaker as it passes over Delaware, Maryland, New Jersey, and New York. FEMA **employees** open emergency centers in Philadelphia and New York City. Teams of doctors and search-and-rescue workers help along the coast. Teams begin to see how bad the damage is in Florida. Many shelters in Florida close as people go home, but Georgia has 18,053 people in shelters, South Carolina has 43,661, and North Carolina has 37,354.

NEWS BULLETIN

September 17—Floyd moves over Connecticut, Rhode Island, Massachusetts, and Maine and then into Canada. Helicopters, airplanes, and boats help with rescue work. North Carolina needs the most help with search-and-rescue and communications. Emergency supplies are sent there. Emergency water is sent to Virginia. Teams look at damage in North Carolina and plan to go the other states soon after. Nearly one and a half million homes are without power. Only about 12,000 people are still in shelters. Almost 2,500 federal workers are helping.

Know It

Project Impact preparations helped in different ways in different places. In New Hanover County, North Carolina, the preparations greatly helped. No **communications systems** failed, and people evacuated quickly and easily. In Freeport, New York, buildings along the coast had been raised above flood heights. They stayed dry even during the terrible flooding from Hurricane Floyd.

Shelters were set up in schools. Because so many people needed shelter, beds even lined the hallways.

Emergency supplies were sent where they were needed most.

This power station was flooded, but power was sent around it and still made it through.

A Closer Look: National Flood Insurance Program

One way to help people after a disaster is by giving them money to rebuild their homes and businesses. Sometimes that money comes from **federal** or state grants, which are gifts of money. Some emergency money comes from **insurance** policies. People buy insurance for most kinds of disasters, from hurricanes to earthquakes. The most common risk for damaging **property** is flooding. FEMA has special programs to help **victims** of flooding.

First, FEMA makes maps so people know if their property is on a **floodplain**. Second, FEMA helps **mitigate** against property damage by moving buildings too close to flood risks away from the risk. FEMA officials also write guidelines on how to manage a floodplain so that the risk of harm is lessened. When community leaders follow these guidelines, they protect lives and property. They can also buy special flood insurance from FEMA and private insurance companies.

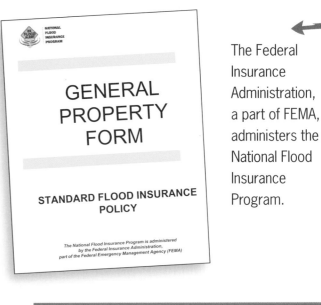

NATIONAL FLOOD INSURANCE PROGRAM

GENERAL PROPERTY FORM

STANDARD FLOOD INSURANCE POLICY

The National Flood Insurance Program is administered by the Federal Insurance Administration, part of the Federal Emergency Management Agency (FEMA)

The Federal Insurance Administration, a part of FEMA, administers the National Flood Insurance Program.

This church, which had been flooded several times over the course of five years, is being moved 500 feet (152 meters) from its original position and out of harm's way.

About 19,000 communities are a part of the National Flood Insurance Program. Because the guidelines work so well, about $800 million is saved each year from damage. The guidelines also give advice on how to build stronger buildings. These suffer much less damage in a disaster than buildings that don't follow the guidelines.

Victims of the 1997 Red River Valley flood inspect the damage to their homes.

Responding to a Disaster

FEMA sets up emergency food centers and shelters to provide help to victims of earthquakes.

The American Red Cross and Salvation Army also step in to help FEMA with disaster relief for victims of natural disasters.

When a disaster strikes, FEMA **employees** work with local and state governments to get help where it is needed. A local emergency plan should help people get started. Most disasters need special stations. Some are **shelters** for **victims** who can't go back to their homes. These stations provide food, water, and clothes and blankets. Some stations have **communications systems** that help people know what's going on.

Other stations are **triage** units. When people get hurt in a disaster, they are taken to triage. Those who are hurt the worst are treated first. To treat people, hospitals are put on alert. Sometimes people can't get to hospitals, so doctors and nurses set up medical stations at the disaster and help people there.

FEMA employees work with other organizations to help during a disaster. The American

Red Cross creates a list of missing and found people so that citizens can find their family members and friends. Red Cross workers also give out food, water, and clothing.

Many **federal agencies** work together when a federal disaster is declared. They use the Federal Response Plan to bring teams in to help. These teams may include doctors and workers who can identify unsafe places. Some workers search for survivors and rescue them. Some teams fix electricity systems. Other teams clear wreckage from collapsed buildings. Another team brings in large kitchens to cook for victims and water purification units that make water safe to drink. Even portable toilets and showers are needed.

Know It

FEMA often uses special mobile units to help during a disaster. These Mobile Emergency Response Support teams help people on site take care of the emergency workers, make decisions about what to do next, and keep information moving to people who need it. All this saves lives by helping workers work together.

After an earthquake, fire is a great risk. Emergency workers must turn off power and gas supplies.

Trucks like these can be driven or even flown into a disaster site. They help with the rescue missions as well as provide communication between emergency and rescue workers.

A Closer Look: September 11, 2001

FEMA has a system of 28 Urban Search-and-Rescue Teams across the United States. All team members must be able to give emergency medical help. Some members are engineers who know how to make unsafe buildings safe. Others are searchers who work with **sniffer dogs** or special cameras. Some team workers are doctors who know how to set up field hospitals. Each team has 62 members. Each job in the team has two people to fill it, but only one works at a time. That way, workers can switch off if they need to. They work for twelve hours then have twelve hours off. Usually a team works for no more than a week before being sent home.

Between shifts, these Urban Search-and-Rescue Team workers take a break. Some of the equipment they use is on the floor around them.

After the **terrorist** attacks on the World Trade Center and the **Pentagon** on September 11, 2001, FEMA immediately stepped in to help. Eight Urban Search-and-Rescue Teams started working at the World Trade Center and four at the Pentagon, near Washington, D.C. They started by helping the local rescue workers decide how to search for people trapped in the wreckage. They tried to figure out where **victims** may have been trapped. Then they began to search, using cameras, listeners, and dogs to help them. When victims were found, the medical people treated them.

The World Trade Center made more than 1 million tons of rubble, so searching through it was very hard. As the rubble was made safe, the searchers looked deeper. Slowly, the teams lifted layers of rubble off the sites,

Dogs help sniff for people in the rubble. They are important members of the rescue team.

It was a difficult and time-consuming task to search through so much rubble at the World Trade Center site.

mostly by hand. Using large cranes or tractors can make wreckage unsteady, so the rescuers set up lines of people to pass buckets of rubble away.

Along with the search and rescue, FEMA helped in other ways after the disaster. About 3,500 **federal** workers were involved. Some helped victims find out what **benefits** or help they could get. Others helped decide what to do with all the money donated by people wanting to help. Many people went door to door in the neighborhoods around the World Trade Center, talking with people and listening to their worries, and trying to help as they could.

People kept searching through the World Trade Center rubble, even during the night. It took over eight months to clean up the rubble. A special ceremony was held on May 31, 2002, to mark the end of the task.

Recovery After a Disaster

When the shock of a disaster begins to go away, people start to think about what will happen next. Often this recovery work begins while the rescue work is still going on. After big disasters, the recovery process can take years to finish.

An important part of recovery is **crisis counseling**. After a disaster, people can be scared and very sad. Many people lose members of their families or their friends in a disaster. These people may have great feelings of grief. Crisis counselors are workers who are trained to help people deal with these feelings.

Citizens who survive a disaster must then take care of their homes and **property**. FEMA officials help set up special stations to tell people how to get money to help rebuild. Local governments can get help rebuilding public buildings, roads, and bridges. Some money is given as **loans** that need to be paid back. Some money is given as grants, which are gifts that do not need to be paid back. People who have lost their jobs because of the disaster can get money to help them live.

To get help, citizens can call special telephone help lines or can visit special centers created near a disaster. Some people need help to make their homes safe to live in or stronger so they can withstand another disaster. Other people need help finding new homes in which to live. They may be able to stay in **shelters** for a while, but then they will need a permanent home.

People can apply for help after a disaster in person or over the telephone.

Cleaning up after a disaster can be hard work, but people can feel good about helping their community rebuild.

During and after a disaster, people with pets worry about how to care for them. Most disaster shelters won't take pets. Some people can make a room safe in their house for their pets to live in, with water and food to last a few days. Sometimes, animal shelters take care of pets during and after a disaster.

It is a wonderful feeling when your whole family, including your pets, are safe after a disaster.

A Closer Look: Northridge Earthquake

The Northridge earthquake in California in 1994 is one of the largest recovery efforts in which FEMA has been involved. The earthquake cost more than any other natural disaster—about $25 billion in damage. About 114,000 buildings were damaged and 11,846 people were hurt. Seventy-two people died.

FEMA gave money to help citizens rebuild and find places to live, pay for their lost wages, and pay for **crisis counselors.** Money also helped rebuild public buildings and roads. Experts then helped citizens how to rebuild wisely so the next earthquake wouldn't cause as much damage.

Schools in the area received more than $2 million in 1996 to **mitigate** against damage from future earthquakes. Ceilings and ceiling lights in schools were fixed to make them safe if the buildings shook. Concrete walkways, bridges, and stairways were rebuilt to survive another earthquake. Between mitigation and repair money, schools in the area received more than $118 million.

Hospitals were given more than $3 million to make buildings and spaces inside safer in case of another earthquake. This money also helped prepare them to be community centers in times of disasters. Overall, hospitals

The Northridge earthquake destroyed many houses and apartments. The outside walls of this building fell, leaving the inside exposed.

Some bridges collapsed during this earthquake, so traffic was unable to move.

received almost $9 million after the earthquake.

Since 1971, leaders in California have been working to support older bridges with new **technology** to make them stronger. This is called retrofitting. Before the Northridge earthquake, more than 1,000 bridges were retrofitted. After the earthquake, the retrofitted bridges had little damage. The bridges that were damaged the most were those that had not yet been retrofitted. More than 1,000 bridges were added to the list to be retrofitted after the earthquake.

Some people were given short-term **shelter** in tents.

FEMA's Workforce

Many Americans think that FEMA **employees** are the first people on the scene of a disaster, helping to save people's lives in daring rescues. Most often, state and local workers are there first. FEMA workers arrive later to help organize rescue missions and the many other jobs of handling a disaster.

After a disaster, FEMA employees in all kinds of jobs work very long days, with no time off. They are used to getting calls at home on weekends and at night to come help in a disaster. Even though this kind of work can be very tiring, it also gives FEMA workers great satisfaction. They know that the work they do helps people when they most need it.

All government **agencies** have personnel who work in the FEMA headquarters.

FEMA has specialized jobs. Specialists include engineers, architects, teachers, people who work with **Congress** and foreign governments, and **public affairs** workers. Some employees work as emergency managers. Emergency managers mostly work with state and local leaders. They give emergency response training to citizens, teach people about new emergency plans, and show builders how to design safer buildings. They also help train people to use specialized equipment, such as hazardous materials response equipment.

FEMA environmental scientists discuss how to handle a disaster in North Carolina.

FEMA also has **geologists** and environmental scientists. Environmental scientists study how land use can make the risk higher or lower for a natural disaster. For instance, they study how a river is being used and where houses are planned to be built along the river. Then they advise community leaders on how to keep the homes and other **property** along the river safe from floods.

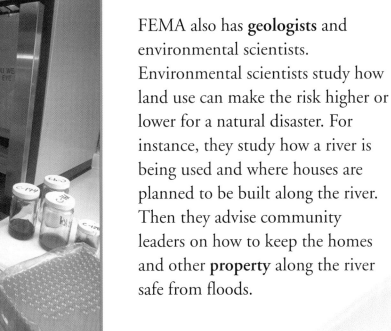

This scientist helps in clean-up efforts that followed the devastating floods that hit the Midwestern states in June 1994.

A Closer Look: FEMA Engineer

Mike Buckley is the Division Director for Hazard Mapping. He works with a team of 25 people at FEMA headquarters in Washington, D.C. He is in charge of making maps of all the **floodplain** and earthquake zones in the United States. His team works with engineers at headquarters and at the regional offices.

The white arrow shows how much land can be covered in water when this area floods.

Mike is a **civil engineer.** He has worked for FEMA for more than 20 years. Most of the people he works with are also engineers. Some are FEMA **employees,** but others work for private companies. These companies are hired by FEMA to help make the hazard maps.

To make a floodplain map, for example, a company is hired to do the field study. Engineers measure features like mountains and rivers. They show how water flows over the land. They also look at historical records to learn about floods long ago. Then they put all the information into a computer. The computer helps make a model, or picture, of the land. This model maps the floodplain and then uses all the measurements gathered and the historical information to predict what might happen in a flood.

It takes about two years to make the floodplain map. Citizens who live in the area that is being mapped look at the map and ask questions. Mike's team makes final changes and completes the map. There have been about

20,000 hazard maps made since 1968. After land is developed or floods happen, the maps must be updated.

Mike spends his days talking to government officials and developers and answering their questions about hazard maps. He goes to meetings with other government **agencies** and outside companies. He works with many people to improve the mapping program.

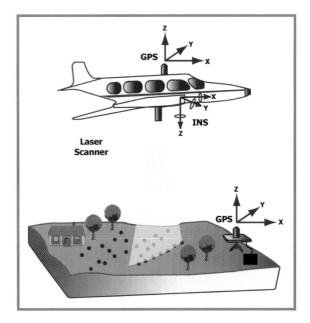

A special airplane uses light beams bounced off the ground to read all the features of the land.

Sometimes Mike works on a disaster site. Floods can change the topography of land. Floodplain maps must then be updated after a flood. This work needs to be done before the recovery work can start so people don't build in dangerous places. Mike even helped in Argentina after a flood. The Argentine government asked for help with **mitigation** plans and in setting up their own agency like FEMA.

The information the airplane has gathered is used to make a floodplain map, showing the normal way the river runs and where it would flood if it gets too full.

A Closer Look: Disaster Assistance Employees

Luckily, FEMA does not have to work on major disasters every day of the year. Because of this, FEMA only needs many extra people during major emergencies. These important temporary workers are called disaster assistance **employees,** or DAEs. These workers must be able to leave their regular jobs and go to disaster areas in one day. DAEs perform many types of jobs. They help plan rescue and recovery missions, work with governments and **media,** give advice on safe ways to work, train other FEMA employees, inspect damage, talk with **victims,** keep communications open, and help make financial plans.

Vanessa Villery has been a DAE for seven years and has worked on more than eighteen disasters. She is a community relations specialist. She is part of the emergency response team, which means she goes to an emergency two hours after she gets the call to go. Some years she works almost full-time for FEMA, and in other years she has few calls. She usually works for one to four months on the job. This makes it difficult for Vanessa's family, especially her daughter, who misses her mother when she is away.

A FEMA worker helps a girl displaced by the Northridge earthquake.

A FEMA community relations worker listens to the needs of New York residents after the **terrorist** attacks of September 11, 2001.

DAEs set up this field office after floods devastated parts of the Midwest in 1994.

DAEs and other FEMA workers spend a lot of time together during difficult situations. They often see each other at different disasters, and become close friends. While they are working at disaster sites, they stay in hotels and eat in restaurants. When they arrive at a disaster, they begin working with citizens in the communities in the area. They don't take control over the site, but instead work to help the citizens.

When Vanessa gets to a disaster, she usually helps to set up the field office. Vanessa is often the field coordinator. She **analyzes** the situation by looking at how much money is available and how many people need help. She must also decide which areas are most damaged. Then she gives workers their jobs. Some workers go into the community and help citizens understand how FEMA can help with grants and **loans.** Vanessa and others work with community groups to help everyone understand how best to survive the disaster. They also talk with people who need more specific help. This information is reported to the field office so the right specialists or machinery can be sent to help.

National Emergency Training Center

The National Emergency Training Center occupies a former college campus in Emmitsburg, Maryland. Two separate training schools are based there: the Emergency Management Institute and the National Fire Academy. The campus has housing for students, dining rooms, classrooms, and special laboratories to help **simulate** disasters.

Instructors at the Emergency Management Institute train workers to help during disasters. About 13,500 people—from government officials to emergency managers—come to Emmitsburg each year for training. They learn how to create plans for emergencies and how best to manage a disaster. They also learn how to plan exercises that simulate a disaster so workers can test how ready they are for the real thing. Special classes for architects and engineers teach the newest and best ways to make buildings more able to withstand disasters.

There are also classes for workers who can't go to the campus. Independent study courses can be taken by anyone who wants to be prepared for a disaster and learn how to help during one. Special classes help families learn how to prepare for disasters. Citizens throughout the United States can take workshops and classes by **satellite** television on the Emergency Education Network.

Local officials plan for disasters at the National Emergency Training Center.

Dan Summers is the emergency management director for New Hanover County in North Carolina. His community faces natural disasters almost every year. In 1994, he brought about 50 community leaders to the Emergency Management Institute. In 2002, Dan brought another 70 community leaders to the institute's Mt. Weather, Virginia, campus. People such as the police and fire chiefs, mayors and government officials, hospital and emergency medical workers, company leaders, airport officials, local **military,** and local **media** all went.

They learned how best to use their community's disaster plan. They did three types of exercises to practice skills they would need in a disaster. First they went through a tabletop exercise using telephones to fix problems brought on by the disaster. Next, they practiced how they would respond during a real disaster. Finally they did a complete simulation, using real smoke and fire trucks, with people pretending to be **victims.** They moved the people to safety and worked together like they would during an emergency.

By learning how to work together as a team, they learned how important each person is during a crisis. Dan says, "All disasters are local. It's the local people who manage the disaster and work to recover from it. But we don't do disaster management every day. We do our regular jobs every day. This training helps us get up and running and then maintain our ability to respond well."

Community leaders train together to be better prepared for disasters in their area.

Simulating a disaster can help people prepare for when a real disaster strikes.

United States Fire Administration

The United States Fire Administration, or USFA, works to protect lives and **properties** from fires. USFA workers train firefighters from across the country. They invent new ways to fight and prevent fires. USFA workers also publish information to help people and communities learn how to lessen their risks from fires.

USFA officials also collect **statistics** about fires from across the United States. There are about 32,000 fire departments that report their information to the USFA. This information helps community leaders see how fires are changing. For example, the number of fires has stayed about the same over the past ten years, but the number of people who died and were hurt because of fires has dropped by a large amount. Statistics help managers know what to do to help reduce the risks of fires even more.

The United States Fire Administration keeps fire statistics and publishes materials about fire prevention.

The USFA is located at the National Emergency Training Center in Emmitsburg, Maryland.

Reduce the Risk

The USFA works hard on fire prevention. Many fires can be prevented by doing simple things, such as putting smoke detectors in every home. Fires can get out of control in as little as 30 seconds, so families must be able to act very quickly. USFA officials say that families can help stay safe by doing these things:

- Make an escape plan and practice it every month. Part of the plan should be having a special place to meet outside, away from the house. As soon as people escape, they should go there. That way, everyone will know who is out of the building. One person should be picked to go to a neighbor and call 911.

- Know two ways to get out of every room in the house. Some rooms may need special ladders to get out of windows safely. Practice using each way of getting out of a room—make sure that your windows open properly, and you know what to do to get out.

- If there are security bars on windows, know how to open them quickly.

- Don't try to save any items when escaping from the house. Get everyone out, and let the firefighters work to save the property.

- If families must go through smoke, they should stay low to the floor and cover their mouths and noses. Smoke can have dangerous chemicals in it that can make people dizzy or pass out.

- Feel doors before opening them. If a door feels hot, do not open it.

- Do not go back in to a burning building. Firefighters will be there quickly, and they have the equipment to see and breathe in the fire.

This family is practicing its escape plan, using a folding ladder to get out of a high window.

Smoke detectors should be checked every month to make sure they work. There should be one on every level of the home and one in or outside each bedroom.

A Closer Look: National Fire Academy

This burn lab at the National Fire Academy helps firefighters learn to fight fires better.

The academy's Learning Resource Center houses material that helps people research emergency topics.

The National Emergency Training Center is the home of the National Fire Academy. Instructors here teach classes to firefighting leaders throughout the United States. These students may be senior firefighters, emergency medical workers, emergency fire managers, or fire station managers. Some of the classes teach better ways to fight fires. Some teach how to manage a fires station or an emergency.

Even though more than 1.5 million people have trained at the National Fire Academy since 1975, not everyone can go there. So the academy also has

Instructors help firefighters learn how to make better decisions in an emergency situation.

distance-training classes. Trained instructors work in each state, teaching **volunteer** firefighters and full-time firefighters in the same subjects covered in the on-campus classes.

Classes are free for most students. If they come to the academy, they stay in the dormitories and eat in the dining halls on campus. The academy has special **simulation** labs, such as the **arson** burn lab and a fire prevention lab that helps people learn better ways to stop fires.

How does the National Fire Academy help firefighters?

The assistant chief of the Bismarck, North Dakota, Fire Department thought that his department's training helped them be safer. After a bad fire he wrote, "Before our training, we would have entered that building and fought regardless of safety. Today we 'read' the situation and make decisions based upon what we learned at the National Fire Academy."

Instructors at the National Fire Academy also teach classes in emergency medical skills. The director of emergency medical services in Thompson, Manitoba, Canada, came to the academy for training. He said, "I would like to congratulate you and your staff and the course instructors on providing a truly cutting-edge class unlike any other in North America."

The National Fire Academy is also home to the National Fallen Firefighters Memorial. This honors the firefighters who have died while working to save others.

Keeping People Informed

FEMA works with local communities every day. **Mitigation** efforts, prevention plans, and training for emergency workers all help communities prepare for disasters. But when an emergency does happen, FEMA's **communications system** helps people know what to do. Information during an emergency is very important. Workers and citizens need to know what areas are safe and unsafe, whether they can drink the water, how to get help, and if their friends and family are safe.

The Office of **Public Affairs** at FEMA runs many of the communications methods.

- The Recovery Channel on television provides expert advice, with information on disasters, **shelters,** and cable and **satellite** stations and briefings on what will happen next in the area. After the Northridge earthquake, 680,000 **victims** watched the Recovery Channel.

The Recovery Times is a very useful newsletter for people in a disaster area.

- *The Recovery Times* is a special newsletter with articles about the disaster and advice on how to cope and rebuild.

- The FEMA Radio Network helps local radio stations get expert interviews and FEMA information out to listeners.

- FEMA FAX lets people call in for more than 2,000 different faxes about disasters, and also sends out faxes during disasters to the emergency workers.

- The FEMA Internet web site keeps citizens up-to-date during disasters with the latest news. It also keeps a library of information about past disasters.

During a disaster, people who are managing the rescue effort need accurate weather reports and communications. This kind of clear communication helps communities get working again as quickly as possible. FEMA can bring in mobile communications systems complete in trucks or in parts by airplane or helicopter. FEMA can also fly a **military** plane to the site to act as a disaster management center in the sky.

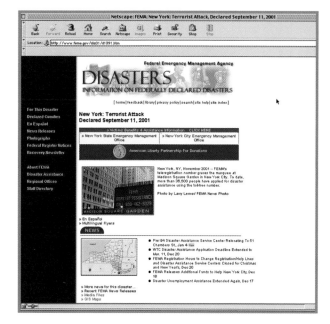

More than 3 million people go to the FEMA web site every week.

Some natural disasters, like tornadoes, are hard to predict. Earthquake prediction is getting better. Hurricanes are the easiest to track, since they usually follow a curving course.

Hurricane watch

At the beginning of hurricane season, weather experts predict how many storms will hit the United States. As each storm develops, tracking its progress and predicting its moves each day becomes very important. The National Weather Service and the National Hurricane Center work closely with FEMA to make sure this important information is sent to people who need it.

Long Term Goals

FEMA officials work to improve how they help people prevent disaster and respond during one. Like all government **agencies,** FEMA has created a plan to keep getting better. It updates the plan regularly, talking with officials in other agencies, states, local communities, Native American people, and **Congress** to make sure it is meeting their needs.

United States Fire Administration officials also make goals and works to meet them. They want fewer people to die in fires each year. USFA officials plan to help 2,500 communities and fire services work to reduce the risks of fire in their areas. They also work to respond when new ideas and problems come up.

FEMA works closely with state and local governments to help them protect their communities. It uses money from Congress to do its work. Disasters happen without warning and with different amounts of damage. The **terrorist** attacks on September 11, 2001, were an example of how terrible disasters can be. But FEMA will always be there to respond as best it can, working with its partners to make the most effective rescues and future prevention efforts.

FEMA's Goals

Goal 1: Protect people and **property** from disasters. This goal is based on **mitigation** and prevention. FEMA wants communities and public services to be much better at resisting the destructive force of natural disasters. Part of this effort is helping more communities take part in the National Flood Insurance Program. Over half of FEMA's strategic money and effort is going into this goal.

Goal 2: Help people suffer less and

This house, originally built in a flood zone, was raised a level to protect it from future flooding.

recover more quickly after a disaster. FEMA is working to make better response methods after a crisis so people are rescued faster. Getting people out of wrecked buildings and dangerous situations fast helps them heal faster. Helping people find their families and friends as quickly as possible helps them worry less. When all the people are rescued, giving communities good advice and help to rebuild fast and better than they were keeps people looking to the future with hope.

Search-and-rescue team members comb through rubble after a gas-line explosion destroys a building in San Juan, Puerto Rico.

Goal 3: Help the public as quickly and as well as possible. This goal means FEMA wants to be as efficient and helpful as possible when people come to it with questions, for information, or for assistance.

FEMA provides personal assistance to help community members deal with the huge task of recovery following a devastating disaster.

Naming Hurricanes

There may be several hurricanes moving across the ocean at once, so hurricanes are given names to help identify which storm is which and track them as they travel across the ocean or hit land.

But why are hurricanes named after people? The tradition of naming hurricanes after people began hundreds of years ago in the West Indies. Followers of the Catholic religion there celebrated a particular saint almost every day of the year. These were called "feast days." Whenever a hurricane occurred, it would be named after the saint whose feast day it was. In the early 1950s, the U.S. National Weather

In this satellite image, Hurricane Floyd is shown nearing the coast of Florida.

Service, the **federal agency** that tracks hurricanes, began using only women's names for hurricanes. In 1979, male names were introduced.

Today, the World Meteorological Organization uses six different name lists for hurricanes in the Atlantic Ocean. The lists are used in rotation. So, the 2003 list will be used again in 2009. Each list contains names for every letter of the alphabet, except *Q, U,* and *Z.* For hurricanes that occur in the Atlantic Ocean, names that are French, Spanish, or English are used, since the majority of countries that border the Atlantic Ocean use these languages. Hurricanes in other parts of the world use different name lists.

Sometimes a name may be dropped from the World Meteorological Organization's list if a hurricane with that name caused a great deal of destruction to homes and **property** or took many lives. When this happens, the name is retired and replaced with a new name for that letter.

Name Lists for Atlantic Ocean Hurricanes

2001

Allison Barry Chantal Dean Erin Felix Gabrielle Humberto Iris Jerry Karen Lorenzo Michelle Noel Olga Pablo Rebekah Sebastien Tanya Van Wendy

2002

Arthur Bertha Cristobal Dolly Edouard Fay Gustav Hanna Isidore Joesephine Kyle Lili Marco Nana Omar Paloma Rene Sally Teddy Vicky Wilfred

2003

Ana Bill Claudette Danny Erika Fabian Grace Henri Isabel Juan Kate Larry Mindy Nicholas Odette Peter Rose Sam Teresa Victor Wanda

2004

Alex Bonnie Charley Danielle Earl Frances Gaston Hermine Ivan Jeanne Karl Lisa Matthew Nicole Otto Paula Richard Shary Tomas Virginie Walter

2005

Arlene Bret Cindy Dennis Emily Franklin Gert Harvey Irene Jose Katrina Lee Maria Nate Ophelia Philippe Rita Stan Tammy Vince Wilma

2006

Alberto Beryl Chris Debby Ernesto Florence Gordon Helene Isaac Joyce Keith Leslie Michael Nadine Oscar Patty Rafael Sandy Tony Valerie William

Retired Hurricane Names

Agnes Alicia Allen Andrew Anita Audrey Betsy Bob Camille Carla Carmen Celia Cesar Cleo Connie David Diana Donna Elena Fran George Gilbert Gloria Hortense Janet Joan Louis Marilyn Mitch Opal Roxanne

Further Reading

Chambers, Catherine. *Earthquakes.* Chicago: Heinemann Library, 2000.

Chambers, Catherine. *Floods.* Chicago: Heinemann Library, 2000.

Chambers, Catherine. *Hurricanes.* Chicago: Heinemann Library, 2000.

Louis, Nancy. *Heroes of the Day.* Edina, Minn.: ABDO Publishing Co., 2002.

Watts, Claire. *Rescue.* New York: Dorling Kindersley Publishing, Inc., 2001.

Glossary

agency part of a government responsible for a certain task

analyze to look at and study something very carefully

arson crime of setting fire to buildings or other property

benefit something that is helpful; help from government agencies

budget plan for spending a certain amount of money in a period of time

civil defense citizens responding to an attack or natural disaster with rescue efforts, and the prevention measures they take before emergencies

civil engineer person who designs and plans large construction projects, such as bridges, canals, dams, tunnels, and water supply systems, as well as airports, highways, and railroads

communications system network of phone lines, computers, faxes, satellites, and other kinds of machines and wires that lets people talk to each other and share information

condemn to order to be shut down

Congress main lawmaking group in the United States, made up of separate houses of senators and representatives

crisis counseling helping people come to terms with their losses and how their lives change after a disaster

directorate division or department within an organization

electric generator machine that supplies electricity

employee worker for a company or organization

evacuated removed from a place that is dangerous to a place that is safe

federal describing a union of states that share a government

floodplain low, flat land that sometimes floods

forecast to predict after studying available facts

geologist scientist who studies the history and structure of the earth

hazardous waste very dangerous garbage or used chemicals that are not needed

hostage crisis situation in which people have been captured and are not allowed to go free

information technology ways of communicating information using computers, phones, and wires

insurance policies protection against damage to property or one's health, agreed to in a contract in paid for with money

invasion act of entering another country in order to take control

loan money or something else that must be repaid or returned

46

media newspapers, magazines, Internet, books, radio, and television stations – all the things that gather and share information and news

military anything having to do with the armed forces

mitigation trying to prevent disaster damage from happening by taking steps to make land and buildings safe

nuclear power plant building in which atomic energy is converted into electricity

Pentagon headquarters for the United States military, located just outside Washington, D.C.

policy accepted way of doing something

presidentally declared disaster disaster that causes so much damage that the president gives permission for the U.S. government to give money and aid

property something that is owned, like a house or land

public affairs work within an agency or company that deals with citizens and people outside the organization

region area that is part of a larger area

retrofit work on something that already exists, like a bridge, to make it safer by adding new parts to it or changing it, instead of knocking it down and rebuilding it

satellite object put into space by people used to communicate or take pictures of the earth

shelter place with heat, food, water, and places to sleep where people or animals can go during a crisis to be safe

simulate to re-create conditions and situations that let people safely practice a job or skill; such a re-creation is called a simulation

sniffer dog dog specially trained to smell and locate certain materials or people

software computer program designed to perform a certain task

statistics facts about a subject or event that are collected in the form of numbers

technology use of science and research to improve life

terrorism use of violence for political reasons, people who do this are called terrorists

toxic poisonous

triage sorting disaster victims or large groups of people in need in order of how quickly their injuries need to be treated

victim person who is hurt by a person or event, such as a disaster

volunteer person who offers his or her help for a short period of time and is usually not paid for the work

Index